Michelle Obama

Barack Obama

Two Biographies

by Joy Brewster

Table of Contents

BIOGRAPHY

What is a biography?

A biography is a factual retelling of another person's life. The person may have lived long ago or in recent history, or the person may still be alive today. Biographies can cover a person's entire life, or just important parts of a person's life. When possible, a biography includes direct quotes from the person. This helps the reader make a connection to the person.

What is the purpose of a biography?

A biography helps a reader understand the people, places, times, and events that were or are important in the subject's life. It provides a summary of the person's major life experiences and achievements. In addition, the way the author writes the biography helps a reader get a sense of the person as a real human being who had (and perhaps still has) an impact on the lives of others.

How do you read a biography?

The title will tell you the subject of the biography and may include something interesting about him or her. The first paragraph will try to "hook" the reader by capturing his or her attention. As you read, note the setting. The setting often influences what happens in a person's life. Also pay close attention to the sequence of events in the person's life. Ask yourself: *Did this event happen to the person, or did the person make it happen? How did this event affect the person's life? What do I admire about this person? Is there something in this person's experiences that I could apply to my life?*

A biography tells the person's date and place of birth.

A biography starts with a strong "hook."

A biography tells about the person's family, childhood, and important events.

Features of a Biography

A biography describes the person's impact on the world.

A biography describes the person's personality and characteristics.

A biography quotes the person and/or people who knew the person.

Who writes biographies?

People who write biographies want to learn more about others' life stories and how those people made their marks on the world. Some people write biographies because they are interested in a certain topic, such as sports, history, or cooking. Others write biographies simply because they are interested in people!

Michelle and Barack

Barack Obama is born on August 4 in Honolulu, Hawaii.

Barack graduates from Columbia University.

Michelle and Barack meet while working at the law firm of Sidley Austin.

Michelle graduates from Harvard Law School.

Michelle and Barack marry.

1961 1964   1983   1985   1988   1991   1992   1993

Michelle Robinson is born on January 17 in Chicago, Illinois.

Michelle graduates from Princeton University.

Barack graduates from Harvard Law School.

Michelle's father dies. She is appointed an assistant to the mayor of Chicago.

Michelle leads Public Allies Chicago, an organization providing leadership training to young adults.

Tools Writers Use
A Strong Lead

A strong lead, or first few sentences, grabs or "hooks" readers. A strong lead makes readers want to keep reading. The lead tells you something important about the subject and hints at what you may learn. Writers use two types of leads. A direct lead tells who or what the piece is about and why the subject is important. An indirect lead may quote someone, ask a question, describe a setting, or tell an anecdote, or true story, about the subject.

Obama

The Obamas' daughter Sasha is born.

Barack is elected to the Illinois State Senate.

Michelle begins working for the University of Chicago.

Barack is elected to the U.S. Senate.

Barack begins his run for president.

1996   **1998**   **2001**   **2004**   **2007**   **2009**

The Obamas' daughter Malia is born.

Barack and Michelle become President and First Lady of the United States. The family moves to the White House.

5

Michelle Obama

Michelle Obama is the First Lady of the United States. She is married to President Barack Obama. But she believes her most important job is being a mom. "Our girls, Sasha and Malia, are the light of our lives," she says **softly**. Family has always been important to Michelle.

A Close Family

Michelle was born January 17, 1964, in Chicago, Illinois. Her parents were Fraser and Marian Robinson. Her dad worked at the city water plant. It wasn't always easy. He had a disease called multiple sclerosis.

Michelle and Barack Obama have two daughters, Malia and Sasha.

Fraser walked with canes, but he worked hard. Marian stayed home with Michelle and her big brother Craig. "Dad was our champion, our hero," remembers Michelle.

The family lived in a small apartment in a little brick house. It had only one bedroom. Michelle and Craig

The Robinsons were a typical working-class family. They lived in an apartment in this house on the south side of Chicago.

slept in the living room. The Robinsons were a happy, close family. They ate meals together. They played games and read together. Grandparents, aunts, uncles, and cousins lived **nearby**.

A Successful Young Woman

Michelle and Craig learned important lessons from their parents: Work hard and treat people with respect. They studied hard in school. They earned good grades. They both went to Princeton University in New Jersey. After college, Michelle went to Harvard Law School in Massachusetts. She and other students helped people who could not afford a lawyer.

Michelle's first job was in a big law firm in Chicago. One summer, another Harvard Law student worked in her office. His name was Barack Obama. Michelle was his advisor. They became friends and then fell in love.

Michelle and Barack started dating after he worked at her law firm one summer. They married in October 1992.

On their first date, Barack took Michelle to the movies. He drove an old, rusty car. She saw that he did not care about money. He cared about something bigger: making a difference. Two years later, they married.

Making a Change

Michelle did well as a lawyer. But after her dad died, she decided to make a change. She wanted to give back to her city. She worked in the mayor's office for a few years, trying to bring new jobs to Chicago. Then she got others to help their city. She led Public Allies, a group that helps young people become leaders in their community.

In her next job, she got college students to volunteer in poor neighborhoods. Then she got a hospital to help out in the community. Many people in the community started volunteering at the hospital, too.

Michelle's life was changing in other ways. She had become a mom. She had two daughters: Malia was born in 1998. Sasha was born in 2001. And her husband Barack had entered politics.

First, Barack served on the Illinois State Senate. Then he became a U.S. Senator. It was hard to juggle her jobs and her family, especially when Barack was in Washington, D.C.

Her Husband Runs for President

In 2007, Barack Obama joined the race for President of the United States. Michelle gave speeches around the country. She also met many Americans: military families, working moms, and lots of young people. People liked Michelle. She was smart, funny, and stylish. Most of all, she was caring. She seemed to understand their stories.

Even with a busy schedule, Michelle always made time for her family.

Michelle worked **hard** to help Barack win the election, but she was never away from Malia and Sasha for long. She spent only one night away from home each week. It was a long, hard race. All the hard work paid off. On November 4, 2008, Barack Obama won the election. The Obamas were moving to Washington, D.C.

In a big speech watched by millions of TV viewers, Michelle said that she (and Barack) believed "you treat people with dignity and respect, even if you don't know them, and even if you don't agree with them." During the race for president, Michelle gave many speeches to large crowds.

Life in the White House

Barack Obama became the president in January 2009. Michelle was **very** excited to work on important causes. She hoped to help working mothers and military families. She also wanted to get more Americans to volunteer in their communities.

As always, her biggest cause was still her kids. Michelle wanted Malia and Sasha to have normal lives. The family ate dinner together. Michelle helped the girls with their homework. She put them to bed. When she wasn't there, Michelle's mom lived in the White House to help out.

As First Lady, Michelle continued working for causes she believed in.

11

Michelle and Barack tried to make the White House a fun place for their daughters. After the family moved in, they put a swing set on the South Lawn. The girls' friends came over to play. They got a "First Dog" and named him Bo. True, the girls had an exciting new life, but some things didn't change. Their mom still made them do chores. They made their beds, cleaned their rooms, and set the table.

It was a long way from the little brick house in Chicago to the White House. But Michelle is still inspired by the same thing: her family.

Malia and Sasha's dad is the president, but their mom still makes them do chores.

Analyze the Subject
- What words describe Michelle Obama? Why?
- What are some of Michelle Obama's accomplishments?
- What things are important to Michelle Obama?
- Who or what has most influenced Michelle Obama in her life?

Analyze the Tools Writers Use
A Strong Lead
Look at the lead in this biography.
- The author used both direct and indirect leads. Which part was direct? Indirect?
- Did the lead "hook" you as a reader? Why?
- What did you expect to learn after reading the lead?
- What are some other ways to start a biography?

Focus on Words
Adverbs
Adverbs are words that modify, or give more information about, verbs, adjectives, and other adverbs. An adverb answers a question such as *how, when, where, why, in what way, how much, how many, how often,* and *to what degree.* Make a chart like the one below. What can you figure out about the following adverbs from the biography of Michelle Obama?

Page	Phrase	Word the Adverb Modifies	Question the Adjective Answers
6	says softly		
7	lived nearby		
10	worked hard		
11	very excited		

The title tells whom the biography is about.

Barack Obama

A strong opening paragraph "hooks" the reader. The author uses a quote from the subject at a very important moment in his life that also had a deep, personal meaning. This helps the reader begin to think of Obama as a person, not just the president.

"We are shaped by every language and culture, drawn from every end of this Earth." Barack Obama stood **outside** the Capitol Building in Washington, D.C. He had just taken an oath. He promised to do his best as the forty-fourth President of the United States. His words described the nation he was about to lead. He was also describing himself.

America is a country shaped by many cultures. Like many Americans, Barack Obama is multicultural. He is the son of a black man and a white woman.

Barack Obama became the new President of the United States on January 20, 2009. His wife Michelle and their daughters Sasha and Malia stood with him.

A Boy from Many Worlds

Barack Obama was born on August 4, 1961, in Honolulu, Hawaii. His parents were from different parts of the world. His dad, Barack Obama Sr., was from Kenya, a country in Africa. His mother, Ann, grew up in Wichita, Kansas. The two met in college in Hawaii. They married and had a son, Barack Obama Jr. They called him Barry. When he was two, Barry's dad left Hawaii. His parents **later** divorced.

The author gives the subject's date and place of birth. Basic facts are very important for a biography. The reader needs to know where and when the events occurred. If the events are in the distant past, the reader needs to think about what life was like then. If it is in recent times, the reader might want to think about where he or she was when the events took place.

Barry's mom remarried when he was six. They moved to Indonesia, a country in southeast Asia. Barry learned the language and the culture. At age ten, Barry, his mom, and his baby sister Maya moved back to Hawaii.

The author tells about the subject's early life, his family, and the different places that he lived. Where a person lived has a big influence on how that person sees the world. A biography is the story of a person's life. As with any story, it needs a setting and characters!

In Hawaii, Barry lived with his grandparents. He called them "Gramps" and "Toot." They didn't have much money. But they sent Barry to a top school. They wanted him to get the best education he could. He studied hard, but he also had fun. He liked to bodysurf at the beach and play basketball with friends. Basketball is still one of President Obama's favorite pastimes.

Barack Obama played on his high school basketball team.

Making a Difference

After high school, Barry went to college. He became interested in politics, especially issues about race. He also decided to use his full name, Barack, from his African father.

College also made him realize he wanted to make a difference. He moved to Chicago, Illinois, and helped people in poor communities. During this time, he made the first of many visits to his father's family in Kenya. These trips connected him to his African roots.

The author describes some key events in the subject's life. The reader learns about what matters to Obama. They see how he acted in difficult situations. These events foreshadow his future life in politics.

Barack decided to become a lawyer. At Harvard Law School, he excelled as a student and as a leader. He quickly proved that he could appreciate and defend both sides of an argument.

One summer, he returned to Chicago to work at a big law firm. There, he met a smart young lawyer named Michelle Robinson. After law school, he moved to Chicago. He married Michelle the next year.

He worked as a civil rights lawyer. He helped people who were treated **unfairly** because of their race, sex, or religion.

Barack also taught a class at a law school. And he worked to register voters to give more people a voice in their government.

A Life in Politics

Barack was helping people, but he believed he could make a bigger difference in politics. In 1996, he was elected to the Illinois State Senate. For eight years, he fought for the working families in his neighborhood. He was thinking about his own family, too. Barack and Michelle now had two daughters: Malia was born in 1998 and Sasha was born in 2001.

In 2000, he ran for Congress. He lost but kept speaking out on national issues. In 2002, he spoke against the war with Iraq. He did not believe that war would make the country safer.

In 2004, he gave an important speech supporting John Kerry, the Democrat running for U.S. President. Barack said the American people were more alike than different: "We are one people, all of us pledging allegiance to the Stars and Stripes, all of us defending the United States of America." The speech was a big hit. People across the country were talking about Barack Obama.

The author tells about people who became important to Obama in his adult life: his wife and children. Remember that biographies are about people's personal lives, as well as their accomplishments.

The author includes this important event in Obama's political life. She quotes a speech he made that made him well known. Using actual quotes helps the reader make a personal connection to the subject.

18

That fall, he was elected to the U.S. Senate. He spoke out for American veterans and victims of Hurricane Katrina. He tackled issues like global warming and government spending. He also worked to make the world safer from dangerous weapons.

Most Americans first heard of Barack Obama after his big speech during the 2004 Presidential race.

The Road to the White House

In February 2007, Barack announced he was running for President of the United States. First, he had to win the Democratic nomination. It was a tight race against Hillary Clinton. She was a U.S. Senator from New York and had been the First Lady when Bill Clinton was president. Still, Barack won the nomination in June 2008. Next, he faced the Republican candidate John McCain. During the campaign, Barack shared his ideas for bringing change and hope to America. Some people wondered if he had the experience to lead the country, but most Americans believed in him.

Here is an example of why the subject is deserving of a biography.

On November 4, 2008, Barack Obama was elected the forty-fourth U.S. President. He made history as the first African American to achieve this high office.

The author ends with something to keep the readers thinking about the subject of the biography, and also about how this person's life connects to their own.

When Barack Obama took office in January 2009, the nation faced many challenges. Many people across the country were losing their homes and their jobs. The United States was fighting wars in Iraq and Afghanistan. President Obama asked politicians, world leaders, and the American people to work together. If they did, the new president believed that America's best days were ahead.

On election night in 2008, the Obama family greeted a cheering crowd in Chicago.

Analyze the Subject
- Why is it important to learn about Barack Obama?
- What are some of Barack Obama's accomplishments?
- What things are important to Barack Obama?
- Who or what has most influenced Barack Obama in his life?

Analyze the Tools Writers Use
A Strong Lead
Look at the lead in this biography.
- What type of lead did the author use? Was it direct or indirect?
- Did the lead "hook" you as a reader? Why?
- What did you expect to learn after reading the lead?
- What are some other ways to start a biography?

Focus on Words
Adverbs
Adverbs answer *how, when, how often,* and *to what degree* questions about verbs, adjectives, and other adverbs. Make a chart like the one below. What can you figure out about the following adverbs from the biography of Barack Obama?

Page	Phrase	Word the Adverb Modifies	Question the Adjective Answers
14	stood outside		
15	later divorced		
17	treated unfairly		

How does an author write a
BIOGRAPHY?

Reread "Barack Obama" and think about what Joy Brewster did to write this biography. How did she describe Barack Obama's life? How did she show what he has accomplished?

Decide on Someone to Write About

Remember: A biography is a factual retelling of someone's life. Therefore, you must either interview the person or research his or her life. In "Barack Obama" the author wanted to tell about Mr. Obama's path from being a young boy in Hawaii to becoming President of the United States.

Decide Who Else Needs to Be in the Biography

Other people will likely be an important part of your subject's life. Ask yourself:

• Who was in the person's family?
• Who were the person's friends and neighbors?
• Who did the person go to school with or work with?
• Who helped or hurt the person?
• Which people should I include?
• How will I describe these people?

Person or Group	Relationship to Barack Obama	How They Impacted His Life
Gramps and Toot	grandparents	sent him to a top school; wanted him to get the best education he could
Michelle Obama	wife	loved him; supported his ambitions
U.S. Senate	governing body to which he was elected	gave him a voice for his concerns and hopes for America

Recall Events and Setting

Jot down notes about what happened in the subject's life and where these things happened. Ask yourself:

- Where did the person's experiences take place? How will I describe these places?
- What were the most important events in his or her life?
- What situations or problems did the person experience?
- What did the person accomplish?
- What questions might my readers have about the subject that I could answer in my biography?

Subject	Setting	Important Events
Barack Obama	United States; Indonesia	1. Barack Obama grew up in a multicultural family.
		2. He became a lawyer and married a lawyer with many of the same goals.
		3. He was elected to the U.S. Senate.
		4. He was elected President of the United States.

Barack Obama chose U.S. Senator Joseph Biden to run as his vice president.

Glossary

hard   (HARD) with great effort (page 10)

later   (LAY-ter) after the stated time (page 15)

nearby   (neer-BY) not far away (page 7)

outside   (owt-SIDE) not indoors (page 14)

softly   (SAUFT-lee) quietly (page 6)

unfairly (un-FAIR-lee) unjustly (page 17)

very   (VAIR-ee) extremely (page 11)